William and Kate

The Prince and Princess

by Simone T. Ribke

Content Consultant
Nanci R. Vargus, Ed.D.
Professor Emeritus, University of Indianapolis

Reading Consultant
Jeanne M. Clidas, Ph.D.
Reading Specialist

Children's Press®
An Imprint of Scholastic Inc.

Library of Congress Cataloging-in-Publication Data

Ribke, Simone T.
William and Kate, Duke and Duchess of Cambridge/by Simone T. Ribke; poem by Jodie Shepherd.
pages cm—(Rookie biographies)
Includes index.
ISBN 978-0-531-22548-6 (library binding) — ISBN 978-0-531-22637-7 (pbk.)
1. William, Prince, Duke of Cambridge, 1982—Juvenile literature. 2. Catherine, Duchess of Cambridge, 1982—Juvenile literature. 3. Royal couples—Great Britain—Biography—Juvenile literature. 4. Princes—Great Britain—Biography—Juvenile literature. 5. Princesses—Great Britain—Biography—Juvenile literature. I. Shepherd, Jodie. II. Title.
DA591.A45W55743 2016
941.086092'2—dc23 [B] 2015021142

Produced by Spooky Cheetah Press
Poem by Jodie Shepherd
Design by Keith Plechaty

Printed in China 62

1 2 3 4 5 6 7 8 9 10 R 25 24 23 22 21 20 19 18 17 16

Photographs ©: cover: Chris Jackson/Getty Images; 3 top left: Ken Brown/iStockphoto; 3 top right: Ben Stansall/Getty Images; 3 bottom: Studio DMM Photography, Designs & Art/Shutterstock, Inc.; 4: Samir Hussein/Getty Images; 8: Photoshot/Newscom; 10: Press Association via AP Images; 12: Anwar Hussein/Getty Images; 15: Tim Graham/Getty Images; 16: Anwar Hussein/Getty Images; 19: The Middleton Family/Getty Images; 20: Max Mumby/Getty Images; 23: Rex Features via AP Images; 24: Max Mumby/Getty Images; 27: Clive Rose/Getty Images; 28: Mario Testino/Getty Images; 30 left: John Stillwell/Getty Images; 30 right: Antony Jones/Getty Images; 31 top: Max Mumby/Getty Images; 31 center top: Samir Hussein/Getty Images; 31 center bottom: Leon Neal/Getty Images; 31 bottom: Anwar Hussein/Getty Images.

Map by Terra Carta

Table of Contents

Meet Kate Middleton

Imagine marrying a real prince or princess. You would live in a castle. You would become a prince or princess, too!

That is just what happened to Kate Middleton. She was a **commoner**. That is someone who is not born into a **royal** family. When she married Prince William of England, Kate became a princess.

Kate Middleton was born on January 9, 1982, in Reading, England. That is in the United Kingdom. Kate has a younger sister and a younger brother.

When Kate was growing up, her parents were very wealthy. They sent her to very good schools.

Kate is a nickname. It is short for *Catherine*.

Area enlarged
Atlantic Ocean
North Sea
Ireland
UNITED KINGDOM
Reading
MAP KEY
United Kingdom
City where Kate Middleton was born

ALTIORA PETIMUS
ALTIORA PETIMUS

Kate did very well in school. She got good grades and was a talented athlete. She was even captain of the field hockey team.

In 2001, Kate went to the University of St. Andrews in Scotland. She studied art history. She also continued playing many sports, including tennis.

This is a photo of Kate (front, center) with her field hockey team.

Meet Prince William

Prince William was born on June 21, 1982, in London, England. His grandmother is the Queen of England.

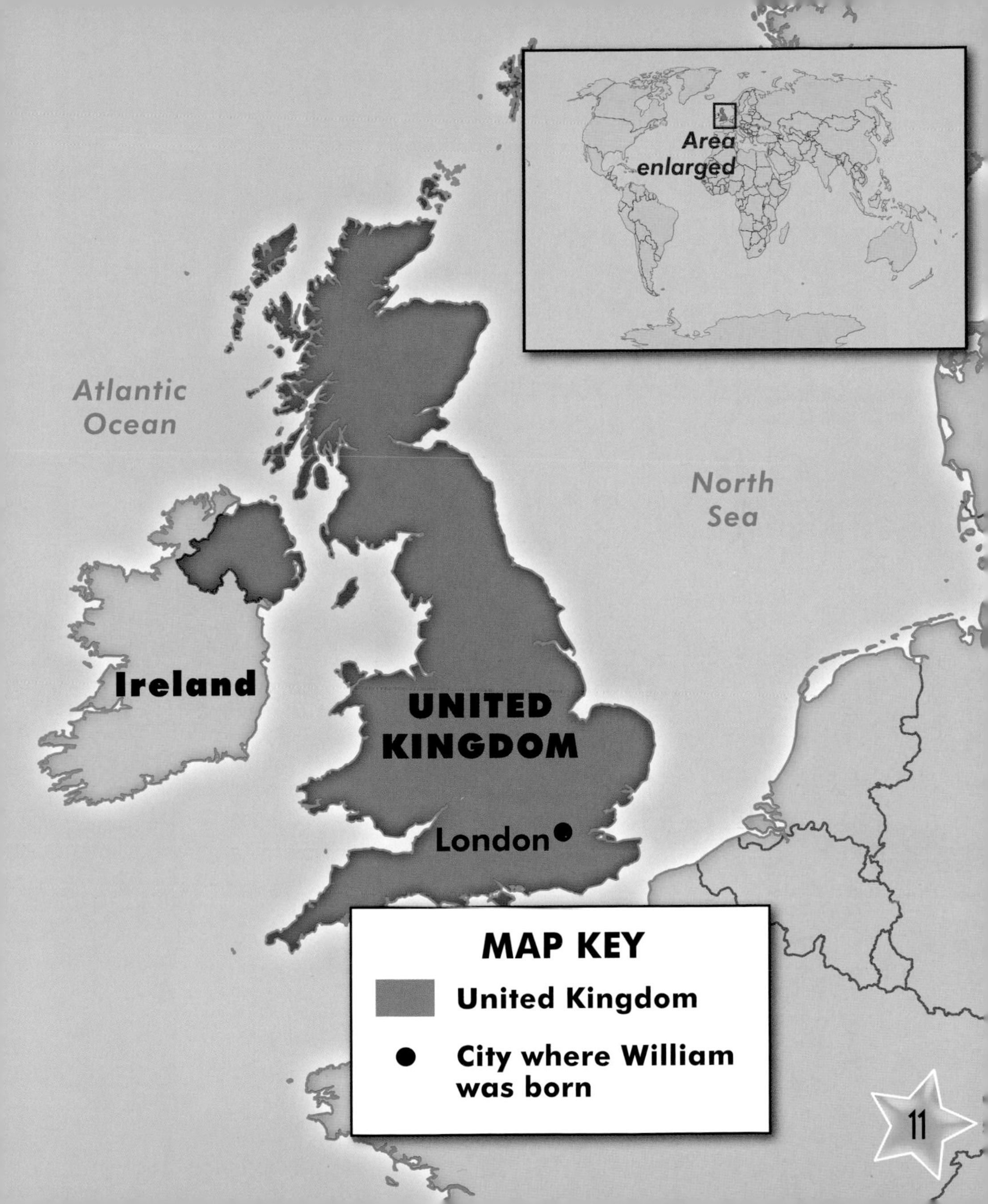
Area
enlarged
Atlantic
Ocean
North
Sea
Ireland
UNITED
KINGDOM
London
MAP KEY
United Kingdom
City where William
was born

Prince Charles and Princess Diana on their wedding day

Prince William is the oldest son of Prince Charles and Princess Diana. When William's parents got married, people were very surprised. Diana was a commoner. It was not usual for a prince to marry someone who did not belong to a royal family.

FAST FACT!

People are very interested in the royal family's life. A lot of photographers follow the family around. Their pictures appear often in newspapers and magazines and online.

As princess, Diana worked hard to help people. She worked for many **charities**. On September 15, 1984, William's little brother, Harry, was born. People all over the world were fascinated by the royal family.

Sadly, William's mother died in 1997, when he was just 15 years old.

This photo shows (left to right) Harry, Prince Charles, four-year-old William, and Princess Diana.

Prince William learned about helping charities from his mother. In 2000, he **volunteered** as an English teacher in Chile. That is a country in South America. The people there said he was very nice and worked hard. Everybody is supposed to call William "Prince William" or "Your Royal Highness." He told the people in Chile to just call him "William" or "Will."

William also helped build walkways while he was in Chile.

William Meets Kate

In 2001, Prince William enrolled in the University of St. Andrews. He and Kate became friends. Soon after, they became boyfriend and girlfriend. But they kept their relationship a secret.

This is a photo of William and Kate at their college graduation.

In 2004, William and Kate took a ski vacation in Switzerland. Photographers took pictures of them. Their relationship was not a secret anymore!

William and Kate ride a "T-bar" ski lift up a mountain.

After graduating from university, Prince William trained in the Royal Air Force (RAF). He learned to fly a helicopter. He flew for the RAF Search and Rescue Force. This team rescues people in danger on land or at sea.

Kate began to work for a clothing company. Then she joined her family's business. She also did a lot of charity work. She tried to keep her life private, but photographers always followed her.

In 2010, William and Kate got engaged. William asked Kate to marry him, and she said yes.

Kate greets children outside a hospital just for kids.

The Royal Wedding

William and Kate were married on April 29, 2011. The wedding was very fancy! The royal couple rode to the wedding in a horse-drawn carriage. Thousands of people lined the streets to watch the parade. Thousands more watched on TV.

FAST FACT!

Prince William is the Duke of Cambridge. When he and Kate married, she became the Duchess of Cambridge.

Timeline of William's and Kate's Lives

1982
Kate Middleton born on January 9

1982
Prince William born on June 21

2001
William and Kate first meet

In 2013, William and Kate started their own family. They had their first child, George. In 2015, they welcomed a daughter, Charlotte.

Their life may seem like a fairy tale. But William and Kate continue to work hard to make a difference in the lives of others.

2010
William and Kate get engaged

2011
William and Kate get married on April 29

2013
George born on July 22

2015
Charlotte born on May 2

A Poem About William and Kate

Kate and Will, Will and Kate,

this royal couple is just great!

They work hard together with lots of grace

to make the world a better place.

You Can Make a Difference

- Lend a hand to someone who could use your help.
- If you are not sure what to do, talk to your parents about how you might help.
- Never stop dreaming.

Glossary

charities (CHAR-uh-teez): groups that help people, animals, or the environment

commoner (KAH-muh-nur): person who is not related to a king or queen

royal (ROI-uhl): related to a king or queen

volunteered (vah-luhn-TIHRD): offered to do a job without pay

Index

Facts for Now

Visit this Scholastic Web site for more information on William and Kate:
www.factsfornow.scholastic.com
Enter the keywords **William and Kate**

About the Author

Simone T. Ribke writes children's books, and she is also an artist. She lives with her husband, children, and schnauzer in Maryland.